Common Sense Rekindled

A Rejuvenation of the American Experiment

Ronald P. Meier

Dear Reader:

Does the future for your children and grandchildren look dismal compared to the future your parents saw for you?

Do your children believe that, when they retire, their Social Security benefits will be non-existent or substantially reduced from today's level of benefits?

Are you afraid that, as you age, even though your life expectancy is far greater than your parents' life expectancy, your health care will be rationed and you will be denied some health care procedures simply because you are too old and must be allowed to die?

Are you afraid of an Islamic terrorist attack greater than 9.11 before you die?

Do you fear that our nation's debt will mean higher taxes on your children and grandchildren and a significant reduction in their standard of living?

Are you afraid that many of America's children are being denied the best educational choices, leaving them ill-prepared for entering the workforce and becoming educated and responsible citizens?

Are you afraid that religious freedom is under attack and that your ability for full religious expression will be greatly reduced?

Does our current pre-WWII level of defense preparedness scare you about our ability to respond to a major terrorist attack?

Are you afraid that America's moral and ethical values are almost lost and not likely to be recovered?

If any of these questions, among many more that could be asked, prompt you to worry about the United States your children and grandchildren will inherit, then read Common Sense Rekindled, endorse the Call to Action, and get moving on the action items. Don't sit and wait for someone to step up and lead you – step up yourself and lead your friends and neighbors.

In 1776, more than half the people in the colonies didn't believe in the cause of the American Revolution; the leaders didn't take a poll to see if they had support for their "call to action." Our current "revolution" need not be violent, but rather in the marketplace for ideas and opinions. If our legislators and government executives are leading "we the people" down the wrong path, they need to be fired and replaced with others who will lead us down the path outlined in Common Sense Rekindled.

If you just sit there and do nothing, your children and grandchildren will receive more of the same!

Table of Contents

Introduction

Thomas Paine, in the Introduction to his highly influential 1776 pamphlet, *Common Sense*, wrote: "Perhaps the sentiments contained in the following pages are not yet sufficiently fashionable to procure them general favor; a long habit of not thinking a thing wrong gives it a superficial appearance of being right and raises at first a formidable outcry in defense of custom. But the tumult soon subsides. Time makes more converts than reason."

Paine's pamphlet brought to the surface emotions long simmering in the hearts and minds of many colonists. Few of them entertained notions of separation from England before Paine's pamphlet was published and distributed. Indeed, time, or perhaps "timing," proved to be more necessary than reason, as many clearly rational reasons for separation had been proposed previously by those inclined to revolution. But, reason alone had proven to be insufficient.

In the early years of the 21st century, we are not beset by the problems of the 18th century. We have no King. We are not colonies of any other sovereign nation. "We the people" are guaranteed certain freedoms in the Bill of Rights and those freedoms have not been formally repealed by Constitutional Amendment. However, those freedoms have been eroded by the courts, by federal regulation and ties to federal mandates, and more importantly by peer pressure from vociferous and powerful groups, even if those groups represent only a small percentage of America's population. "Tyranny by minority" is now a more potent factor in America's culture than the tyranny by majority that our Founding Fathers feared in the 18th century.

Everyone across the political spectrum acknowledges we are a divided nation. In the New Testament, we read in Matthew 12:25: "Every kingdom divided against itself will be ruined, and every household divided against itself will not stand." Even secular Americans, if they have only a shallow understanding of the bible and of world history, and if they consider their own extended families, know and understand the truth of that biblical statement. This is not the first time we've had such division as a nation, nor will it be the last.

Our divisions have generally been more acute on social issues than on economic issues. Today, we are constantly enjoined to focus on solving our national economic and financial issues and to ignore the social issues that divide us. To ignore our social issues is to stick our heads in the sand. Economic stability & growth will not pacify social division.

In the 18th century, life, liberty, and the pursuit of happiness defined our social issues, and those were ultimately resolved with the Bill of Rights. In the 19th century, it was abolition of slavery and the Constitutional Amendments relating thereto. In the 20th century, it was women's suffrage, civil rights, sexual freedom, tolerance, and abortion, among others. In the early stages of the 21st century, our current economic and financial problems are a function of the social welfare programs of Social Security, Medicare, Medicaid, and the social justice aspects of tax policy. Those economic and financial problems cannot be resolved until and unless the social issues are confronted head-on. Religious freedoms, other rights guaranteed by the First Amendment and the right to bear arms guaranteed by the Second Amendment are non-financial social issues causing deep divisions. Those freedoms cannot be pushed to the side, but must be confronted head-on.

Revolution today need not be the armed revolution of the 18th century. Our Constitutional structure already in place is sufficient for resolution of the issues we must confront without resort to armed conflict. But to do so requires active participation by those Americans who, as Paine so eloquently noted, have had "a long habit of not thinking a thing wrong, giving it a superficial appearance of being right" and have passively accepted more than one hundred years of incremental cultural changes that have led America down paths not anticipated by our nation's Founding Fathers.

If "We the People" don't know why our nation is what it is, then "We" will follow our politicians rather than having our politicians follow us. Over the past century, we have followed the politicians; if now is not the time to lead our politicians, when will be the right time? But to lead, we must know where we came from, what caused us to reach prior tipping points, and how we have been led down the path to the current tipping point.

"Experience must be our only guide. Reason may mislead us." So said John Dickinson, Signer of the U. S. Constitution.

The cultural heritage of the United States of America is what made the United States the most successful and prosperous nation ever to inhabit the earth, a beacon to freedom-loving and success-seeking people from every country in the world. As that cultural heritage has changed, particularly since the early 20th Century, and more strongly so since the mid-20th Century, the United States has experienced declining moral and ethical values, a decline in effective political power, and a stagnation and emerging decline in economic and military power.

If the United States is to regain its strengths, it must look to the past to the factors that set in place its emergence as a global power in the 18th Century and rekindle those factors today. Businesses search for "best practices" in other businesses that they can use to replicate the great success stories of other businesses; the identification of political "best practices" can do the same for countries. For more than 200 years, the United States has been the place to look for political "best practices." It has drawn millions to its shores searching for freedom, liberty, and opportunity. If the people of the United States fail to look to the "best practices" of their past, they can expect to experience a continual decline in America's global rankings, similar to what other Republics experienced in the past. Those declines in past Republics have always led to their destruction. As Ben Franklin is reported to have said, "What you have is a Republic, if you can keep it."

Introduction

The United States Constitution begins with the words "We the People of the United States of America." If "we the people" are to know how to resuscitate our country, which each year spends far more than it takes in, increases its national debt at an unsustainable rate, restricts personal freedoms in the name of political correctness, and pursues "social justice" rather than blind justice, then we must know our country's origins and design. We must also know the forces that have been aligned in opposition to our origins and design and understand how those forces will destroy the American Experiment so skillfully designed by Messrs. Washington, Jefferson, Madison, Franklin, and dozens of our nation's other Founding Fathers.

Chapter 1
On the Origins and Design of the American Experiment

What "We the People" Know from Our Nation's History

We accepted the rational and practical elements of the Judeo-Christian Ethic and Morality as the basis of our Nation's Moral & Social Values and for its application to a Republican form of government.

The first settlers in the original colonies were Christian expatriates from Europe. Some suffered religious persecution in their home countries because they disagreed with principles of the state-supported denomination of their homeland; others emigrated for economic opportunity and brought their religious beliefs with them. They established Christian communities for their denominations in America.

Those who emigrated for religious freedom willingly uprooted their families, undertook dangerous voyages across the Atlantic into an unknown environment, where they underwent enormous hardships to survive, just for the freedom to worship God in their own way with other members of their Christian denomination. Certain denominations migrated to different parts of the new world, initially New England and Virginia.

Unfortunately, after they established their colonies, many decreed their own Christian denominations as the official "state-supported" denomination of their respective colonies. Alternatively, if a colony didn't create a state-supported Christian denomination, they decreed that only Christians or Protestants were permitted to hold office. Similar to the experience in Europe, members of other Christian denominations were often persecuted and/or ostracized. The colonists recreated the very same closed religious environment their ancestors left. The table in this webpage shows the state-supported denominations of the various colonies: http://undergod.procon.org/view.resource.php?resourceID=6 9 .

The Great Awakening from 1730-1750 helped start in motion the assimilation of Christian denominations into a more unified Christian body and the eventual decline of state-supported denominations in the Colonies. After the Great Awakening, Colonists became more aware of the power of the unifying factors of the various Christian denominations rather than the distinguishing factors that divided denominations and the Colonies in which each denomination held a majority.

Regardless of denomination, each colony and its citizens recognized the Bible as the source of moral and ethical principles. Protestant Christians in the colonies were 98% of the total population, Catholic Christians 1%, for a grand total of 99%. Christian Biblical moral and ethical principles, therefore, were the driving force underlying the laws of the colonies, rather than man-made secular laws based on logic, reason, and intuition alone. The former lead the culture, are absolute and unchanging, whereas the latter follow the culture, are relative and changing. Ethics and morality were considered necessary for virtuous living and civic virtue, a precondition for the type of society and community ultimately constructed by the Founding Fathers in the Constitution. The Christian Bible was the accepted source of ethics and morality. The Founding Fathers recognized that politics required morality, that religion was the source of morality, and that secular reason is necessary, but not sufficient, for moral judgment.

By the mid-18th century, the Constitutions of the Colonies, their public educational systems, including colleges, and their political structures were all based on Christian morals and ethics derived from the Judeo/Christian bible and Christian tradition.

In addition, the Constitutions of the Colonies contained Bills of Rights, modeled after Bills of Rights developed in the colonies and in England in the 17th Century. The Massachusetts Body of Liberties (1641) is one such example; see http://history.hanover.edu/texts/masslib.html. Another is the 1689 British Bill of Rights; see http://www.legislation.gov.uk/aep/WillandMarSess2/1/2.

Although full religious freedom did not occur in the Colonies prior to the American Revolution, religious freedom underpinned virtually all political declarations of the American Colonists. Christianity provided the colonists the moral vocabulary that defined these political declarations and all colonists knew the source and meaning of that vocabulary.

Collectively, these statements of individual rights, developed over the centuries, heavily influenced, directly and indirectly, the fervor for independence, the Declaration of Independence, the Articles of Confederation, the Constitution, and especially the first 10 Amendments to the U. S. Constitution, titled the Bill of Rights. Full religious freedom was guaranteed by the *federal* government in the First Amendment, but the individual states had state-supported Christian denominations for some years after the ratification of the Constitution and the Bill of Rights. See link above.

With virtually all 18th Century Americans professing Christianity, even though doing so through many different denominations of Christianity, Christianity's moral and ethical values, building blocks for virtuous living and civic virtue, were deemed critical to the longevity of the Constitutional Republic as structured in the U. S. Constitution. John Adams reflected the sentiment of the Founding Fathers when he said "We have no government armed with power capable of contending with human passions unbridled by morality and religion. Avarice, ambition, revenge, or gallantry, would break the strongest cords of our Constitution as a whale goes through a net. Our Constitution was made only for a moral and religious people. It is wholly inadequate to the government of any other."

Chapter 1

The Enlightenment's Impact on the Founding Fathers and Christian Virtue

In the same era preceding the American Revolution, another significant "Great Awakening" had been in process, particularly among the educated elite, which included many of America's Founding Fathers. That was the Enlightenment, which emphasized reason, among other things. Although some saw a great divide between reason and faith, others took the position that reason supported faith and still others took the position that faith supported reason. These different positions naturally created conflicts that exist even to this day.

Among the conflicts, most relevant to this discussion is whether America was founded as a Christian nation, a Secular nation, or something in between. Few would disagree that our Founding Fathers were raised in Christian homes professing orthodox (defined for the purposes herein as one who accepts Jesus Christ as their Lord and Savior and believes in all the elements of the Nicene/Apostles Creed) biblical Christian revelation as truth, were educated in schools which strongly supported their Christian faiths, and were members of a variety of Protestant denominations. Many attended college, which were founded by Christians and supported Christian values and principles, but which increasingly changed with the influence of the Enlightenment's rationalism.

Many of our Founding Fathers saw the need to find a way to rationally apply biblical morality in the creation of a politically moral and virtuous society. They implicitly understood and accepted that religious faith defined the virtues necessary for the type of government they created. However, they had no intention of creating a Christian Theocracy. They recognized that they could not create a political entity based on the religious principles of one of the extant denominations, each of which agreed on a set of core principles, essentially those expressed in the Nicene Creed, but disagreed on certain other denominational principles. Thus they strove to pull from Christian principles and values those that "all good and reasonable men" could agree with and accept (i.e., the moral teachings and lessons), regardless of their beliefs in biblical revelation, the deity of Jesus Christ, and other articles of faith of orthodox Christianity. They reasoned that the rational moral teachings of Jesus were the relevant principles for a civil society; all other principles of the bible were pertinent to specific Judeo/Christian religions and their denominations' traditions.

An example might be instructive. Whereas all orthodox Christians and Jews accept the 10 Commandments as central to their faith, agnostic and atheist Americans, among others, cannot accept those commandments that require worship of a monotheistic Judeo/Christian God. They can rationally accept commandments to not murder, to honor one's parents, to not covet property of another, etc. The Bible's literal and spiritual lessons can be ignored, with only the Bible's moral lessons being extracted.

Some current day authors, particularly Gregg Frazer, author of *The Religious Beliefs of America's Founders*, call this Theistic Rationalism (TR). They posit that our key Founders and others among our Founders, did not attempt to create an orthodox Christian nation, nor a Deist nation; nor did they attempt to create a secular nation, with a "separation of church and state." Rather, they created a nation in which the state protected and encouraged religion in the new nation's public life.

A strictly orthodox Christian nation would require faith and obedience only to God, not to human secular laws, would not tolerate religious beliefs other than Christian, thereby denying religious freedom, and certainly would not tolerate non-belief in a Christian God. The Founding Fathers were affiliated with various Christian denominations, attended services at the church of their Christian denomination, believed that religion was "a crucial support for free societies," but may or may not have adhered to all of the orthodox foundational principles of their denominations. Having been educated in colleges influenced by the Enlightenment, they accepted biblical revelation that was rational, may have accepted some biblical revelation that was purely faith based, and may have rejected other biblical revelation. Frazier posits that even Jefferson and Franklin, who are commonly labeled as Deists, were not Deists because even they accepted some biblical revelation (which they called "Providence") that a Deist would not accept. Frazier states that the term "Deist" was used to label those who couldn't be put into a Judeo/Christian box, yet who also couldn't be put into an agnostic or atheist box.

What Frazier posits is that the renowned Christian evangelists of the Great Awakening period prepared the great majority of non-highly-educated Christians for the highly educated elites of the era, including many college-educated Christian patriotic pastors and preachers, by incorporating Enlightenment rational thinking into their sermons, writings and speeches. Parts of natural religion became combined with revealed religion. With the Enlightenment politicians in attendance at Sunday services and in communication with their pastors, the politicians and pastors were able to intentionally or unintentionally construct consistent messages, without offending religious beliefs, to deliver to the masses in support of revolution and a Constitution that could be accepted by members of all Christian denominations.

The Founding Fathers focused on those elements of Christianity that led to moral and virtuous living and preferred to let the Christian denominations and other religions decide which additional fundamental doctrines they believed necessary for membership and fellowship in each denomination and religion. The Founding Fathers believed that a religion must stimulate a person to good conduct as a citizen and that that Christianity's non-fundamental precepts provided such stimulation. All understood that Christianity defined the duties of man to man. God's role in public life was to lead political actors to promote moral, ethical, and virtuous lawmaking and living. Living morally was sufficient for political living in a community containing people of many faiths, even if not sufficient for acceptance in God's Kingdom.

Chapter 1

Religious Education as the Source of Moral Principles for Civic Virtue

In the summer of 1787, during the proceedings of the Constitutional Convention, the Continental Congress passed the Northwest Ordinance, which was later reaffirmed by the new U. S. Congress and signed into law by President Washington. Article III of the Northwest Ordinance stated that "Religion, morality, and knowledge being necessary to good government and the happiness of mankind, schools and the means of education shall forever be encouraged." Thus, both the Continental Congress and the U. S. Congress formed under the new U. S. Constitution formally confirmed Judeo Christian ethics and morality as a critical component of life in the new nation. Key components in that Judeo Christian ethics and morality were love of neighbor and charity. In the 18th Century, everyone understood that the term "religion" meant Christianity, even if each one viewed religion from his denominational perspective. Schools were considered the optimal training ground for the religious moral and ethical precepts necessary for citizens in a civil society, particularly one with a republican form of government. The religious training in the schools would help transform the naturally self-centered human into an other-centered human with the civic virtue and responsibility necessary for thriving in a republican form of government.

Thomas Jefferson and Benjamin Franklin are believed to be the two least "religious" among the Founding Fathers. Yet, many times both proclaimed in their writings and speeches the necessity of Christianity's values and principles as a guiding light for the new nation. Even they, among the other key founders, believed that God was present and active on earth and in the lives of men, clearly putting them at odds with pure Deists. The many references to "Providence" found in the writings and speeches of America's Founding Fathers are evidence of their belief in a present and active God, even if not necessarily an "orthodox" Christian God. During the difficult political negotiations of the Constitutional Convention, Mr. Franklin pleaded with the participants that each day's proceedings begin with prayer. He did not, however, prescribe the God to whom each person should pray.

Franklin said "I have lived, Sir, a long time and the longer I live, the more convincing proofs I see of this truth -- that God *governs in the affairs of men.*" (A deist did not believe that God was present after creation, but rather that He created the earth and all things in it, and then withdrew from His creation. Thus, it's highly unlikely that even Franklin was Deist.) And "if a sparrow cannot fall to the ground without his notice, is it probable that an empire can rise without his aid? We have been assured, Sir, in the sacred writings that "except the Lord build, they labor in vain that build it. I firmly believe this; and I also believe that without his concurring aid we shall succeed in this political building no better than the Builders of Babel; we shall be divided by our little partial local interests; our projects will be confounded, and we ourselves shall become a reproach and a bye word down to future age. And what is worse, mankind may hereafter this unfortunate instance, despair of establishing Governments by Human Wisdom, and leave it to chance, war, and conquest."

Chapter 1

See http://www.americanrhetoric.com/speeches/benfranklin.htm.

Among Mr. Jefferson's many commentaries on "religion," he said in his 1781 "Notes on the State of Virginia, Query XVIII, "Can the liberties of a nation be thought secure when we have removed their only firm basis, a conviction in the minds of the people that these liberties are of the gift of God? That they are not to be violated but with His wrath?"

George Washington, in his Farewell Address in 1796, said, "Of all the dispositions and habits which lead to political prosperity, Religion and morality are indispensable supports. In vain would that man claim the tribute of Patriotism, who should labor to subvert these great Pillars of human happiness, these firmest props of the duties of Men and citizens. The mere Politician, equally with the pious man, ought to respect and to cherish them. A volume could not trace all their connections with private and public felicity. Let it simply be asked where is the security for property, for reputation, for life, if the sense of religious obligation desert the oaths, which are the instruments of investigation in Courts of Justice? And let us with caution indulge the supposition that morality can be maintained without religion. Whatever may be conceded to the influence of refined education on minds of peculiar structure, reason and experience both forbid us to expect that National morality can prevail in exclusion of religious principle."

Neither then, nor now, has any Christian leader, church, denomination, or organization expressed a desire for a Christian theocracy or even for a nationally supported religious denomination. Our "Theistic Rationalist" Christian

Founding Fathers clearly articulated their rejection of state-supported religious denominations and their acceptance of freedom of belief and worship for adherents of all religious denominations, including atheism. However, our Founding Fathers did recognize that church and state are mutually supportive institutions, with a mutual commitment to order and civic discipline and that the elimination of church from the public square would destroy a critical pillar supporting the foundation of the civic structure of the new Republic. They clearly recognized and acknowledged that "morality without God was an empty cup to be filled with anything man wants."

Chapter 1

Church and State: Separate or Supportive?

At the time of the Constitutional Convention, many colonies had a religious test for holding office in the state. While the Founding Fathers recognized the importance of religious faith to civic virtue, they did not want to create a Christian theocracy; nor did they want to restrict the new Republic's political leadership to believers of only one faith or one denomination within a faith. They wanted a Republic that would protect the rights of people of all faiths and keep America a haven for anyone seeking religious liberty. Therefore, they wrote in Article VI of the Constitution that "no religious test shall ever be required as a qualification to any office or public trust under the United States."

Their vision was for the federal government to protect religious liberty for everyone but not to discourage (and, in fact, to encourage and support) religious belief for every citizen; the language of the Northwest Ordinance most clearly demonstrates this intent. All Founding Fathers were cradle Christians and could identify common moral principles and values that "all good and reasonable men" could agree upon within the articles of faith of the denominations to which each belonged. Therefore, they naturally believed that, as the nation grew and more faiths were represented, those moral and ethical principles would largely be accepted by followers of non-Christian faiths – and even by followers of no-faith. Recent history has not validated our Founders' assumption.

Much is made by some of one phrase in one of President Jefferson's 1802 letters in which he made reference to the "separation of church and state." Jefferson believed that Judeo Christian moral principles were necessary for good order in a society, but that particular sectarian dogmas should not be dictated by the federal government. Under federalism, Jefferson was unable to prevent the State of Connecticut from doing otherwise.

Most importantly, in the 1802 letter, he was assuring a Baptist denomination in Congregationalist Connecticut that, under *federal* law the Baptist denomination and its members could freely practice their sect of the Christian faith, even if under state law, which supported the Congregationalist denomination, its members might be ostracized for their practice of some Baptist dogmas & traditions and might even be forced to pay taxes to the state-supported Congregationalist denomination. The "separation" of which Jefferson spoke was not to prohibit any religiously influenced moral or ethical values from government, but to prohibit the federal government from proscribing which god, which religion or denomination thereof, or which practices of worship citizens should follow.

Jefferson believed, as did all the Founding Fathers, that moral and ethical principles and values from Christian and other religions that "all good and reasonable men" could agree upon and accept were necessary to the function of good government. The fact that those principles and values derived exclusively from the Christian religion was a function of the fact that virtually all colonists at the time were Christian. The new nation's "character," therefore, was defined by Judeo Christian moral and ethical principles, principles based on love of and service to others. The moral and ethical principles of religions or sects thereof that are repugnant to that "character" would not have been accepted then and should not be accepted now. Religious or political doctrines that profess slavery, honor killing, superiority of a particular race or gender, or rights granted only by the state, for example, would and should be rejected in America because they do not build virtuous and moral societies.

John Adams stated "Religion I hold to be essential to morals." Although he attended church services in an orthodox Christian church, he believed that there were many paths to God and that it was important for Americans to find commonalities upon which to build virtuous and moral societies. He believed it was important to have religious beliefs and to attend church services, but that the content of those services was not important so long as it made its members more virtuous and not dangerous to society. Love of neighbor and charity are difficult virtues to apply, even for church-attending Christians. How can those virtues be applied by secular citizens who believe that only each individual's reasoning should dictate virtue? Secular reason leads one to become self-centered, not other-centered.

So, love, good deeds and public morality were the standards by which our Founding Fathers judged "religions" and religious "sects." Those which exhibited these characteristics were considered equally worthy of encouragement and support by the new Republic; those which failed to exhibit these characteristics would not have been considered worthy of encouragement and support by the Republic.

It is important to remember that, in the 18th century, the colonies were inhabited primarily by Christians, worshiping the Christian God under the banners of a variety of denominations. So it could be said that America was, and is today, primarily a nation of Christian people, but that America is not a theocratic "Christian nation." Muslims, Hindus, Jews, and the large number of other non-Christian religions represented an insignificant percentage of colonists; thus, when our Founding Fathers spoke of the equality of all religious beliefs, they were primarily addressing the equality of belief of the various Christian denominations, although they would not have excluded non-Christian sects or secular groups so long as those sects and groups shared the same respect for public virtue and morality, demonstrated love of others, produced good citizens, and performed good deeds. They assumed that all religious sects worshiped the same God, which subsequent immigration into the Republic by peoples of many non-Christian sects may have shown to be an incorrect long-term assumption; but had they known the future, they would have adopted the same moral and ethical principles.

America's social and economic success over the past 200 plus years has been a function of a Republican form of government, structured with a Constitution limiting the powers of the national government and providing checks and balances to minimize the concentration of power in any one of the three branches of government. The foundation of that structure was the Judeo Christian Ethic and Morality, without which all our Founding Fathers acknowledged the nation could not survive. Over the past half century or so, the Judeo Christian foundation has been increasingly eroded as Progressives have used the legislature, the courts, and administrative agencies to create a secular nation, reliant solely on man-made ethical rules and relative moral values. The new moral values accept society's drift towards no fixed moral standards and away from the high standards towards which society should strive.

So, how can the people of the United States recover the foundation upon which their nation's social and economic success has grown? America is a nation of largely Christian people, but it also is a Republic, with freedom of religion. Religious minorities are full-fledged citizens free to practice their religious faith or to have no religious faith at all. President Jefferson, in his 1802 letter to the Danbury Baptists, gives us a clue as to what we can do, when he states "that the legitimate powers of government reach actions only and not opinions."

We must return to our roots and national character if our Republic is to not follow the self-destructive course of other great Republics of the past. Our character was derived from Judeo Christian biblical roots, from which principles and values that "all good and reasonable men" could agree upon were abstracted. Rather than scrub those principles and values from our society and replace them with man-made rules having no moral or ethical foundation outside of modern man's self-centered mind, we must search to rediscover those principles that define our national character, strongly encourage religious belief and practice in the private and public marketplace, and specifically identify those religious and ideological "actions" that undermine our national character and that will not be incorporated in our national character, nor into our federal laws. We cannot disallow

17

beliefs, but we can identify and disallow actions and practices that undermine our national character.

Chapter 1

We Created a Government with Limited Powers, Subservient to the People

Government's limited powers were first recognized in the Preamble of the Declaration of Independence. Key features:

- o All men are created with equal rights and equal opportunities to use their gifts and talents to serve others and to pursue their own version of happiness
- o Man's Creator endows them with certain unalienable rights; those rights are not granted by government or by another human and are not negotiable or subject to revocation
  - ▪ Life, from conception to natural death
  - ▪ Individual Liberty
  - ▪ Pursuit of Happiness
- o Government is empowered, not to grant rights, but to secure the dignity of the individual and his unalienable rights.
- o Government derives its just powers from the people, not from a selected segment of the people deemed to have superior intellectual knowledge and therefore prone to use despotic power to legislate away one's unalienable rights.

The Preamble of the Constitution identifies "We The People" as the authors of the Constitution and the delegators of powers to the federal government. Article I of the Constitution identifies the powers the People have delegated to the federal Legislature and the powers formerly exercised by the States that are no longer retained by the States. Article II identifies the powers the People have delegated to the Chief Executive, the President of the United States. Article III identifies the powers the People have delegated to the Judiciary.

The People are guaranteed in Article IV that each State is guaranteed a Republican form of government, the same form of government the Constitution provides for the federal government. The Constitution provides for checks and balances so that none of the three branches of government can concentrate all the powers in one branch of government.

The 85 Federalist Papers were written and published in the newspapers of the day to educate the people on the intent of the Founding Fathers who drafted the Constitution. The people's memories were still fresh with the Revolutionary War fought over the repression of the people's unalienable rights and legal rights by an all-powerful King and Parliament. After the writing of the Declaration of Independence and throughout the fighting with England, the new nation lived under laws designed for a Confederation. The fear of a unified national government's ability to subjugate individual rights with unlimited concentrated powers was so great that the Colonies originally preferred to organize the new states into a Confederation rather than a unified national government. They preferred that most rights be retained by the States and few rights granted to the "national" government.

Chapter 1

    At the time of the writing of the Constitution, these fears remained paramount in the minds of most citizens. The new Constitution rejected a Confederation form of government, based on the difficulties of governing under such a form over the prior years. Citizens feared a "national" government and the Founding Fathers knew that they would have to show the citizens that the checks and balances incorporated in the Constitution along with the intent of limiting the powers of the "national" government would sufficiently restrain the "national" government from infringing on the rights of citizens and the powers of the States to govern their own affairs. The Constitutional Convention meetings were kept secret and neither the States nor the people knew the direction of the proceedings of the Convention. The delegates to the Convention were instructed by the Continental Congress to meet "for the sole and express purpose of revising the Articles of Confederation." As far as the people knew in September, 1787, that was all the Convention had done. When the final draft of the Constitution was presented to the people, an entirely new structure of the federal government had been proposed, "national" in perception to the majority of the people.

    It would take significant effort to "sell" the people on such a structure. The Federalist Papers were the tool used to do so. The 85 articles were written primarily by Alexander Hamilton, who was a major proponent of the new structure and therefore the ideal person to write the articles to assure the people that adequate checks and balances and safeguards were intended by the delegates to the Convention to protect their individual rights and liberties while granting only limited powers to the federal government. The Federalist Papers are important even in the 21st Century to help today's American citizens understand the original intent of the Continental Congress to limit the powers of the "national" government and retain optimal liberty for all U. S. citizens.

The first ten Amendments to the Constitution were added when the State governments and many of the citizens of the States objected to the fact that no such bill of rights was included in the Constitution. Bills of Rights were common in the Constitutions of the States. Mr. Madison, the primary author of the Constitution believed that the Constitution's language sufficiently addressed the rights of citizens and that a separate Bill of Rights was not necessary. "The People" saw differently and the first ten Amendments to the Constitution were added soon thereafter. The history of America since 1787 has demonstrated the wisdom of the people over the wisdom of Mr. Madison with respect to that point. The Bill of Rights most clearly articulates the intent of the people to limit the powers of the "national" government.

Political leaders of the era defined liberty as freedom from tyranny, oppression, and the arbitrary exercise of power. Christians and their pastors and patriotic preachers believed that human liberty was of divine origin, consistent with God's gift of free will to all humans. Spiritual liberty to worship God and political liberty were not considered mutually exclusive. Defense of God's gift required more than mere passive obedience to tyrannical political authority.

John Locke's influence on the revolution and the republican government eventually established was as significant as religion's influence. Although Locke's concepts focused on the voluntary consent of free men, in apparent conflict with Christian duty to a Supreme Being and the Romans 13 admonition to submit to political authority, patriotic preachers effectively linked Locke's concepts with Christian moral doctrine, calling for just rulers, freely elected by men rather than anointed by God.

Locke's concepts of the equality of man and man's right to life, liberty and property found its way into the Preamble of the Declaration of Independence. When men have equal rights to liberty, and when they have been adequately educated about their rights and responsibilities as citizens in a Republic, then they can give their consent to those they've chosen to represent them as political leaders. The natural self-centeredness of humans was transformed into Christian other-centeredness by stressing the individual's civic responsibility for self-preservation of a society and culture. Civil government in the 18th century was not the God-anointed government of the Old Testament, but a human institution. The human institution many experienced was tyrannical and, according to political and religious leaders of the time, one that humans had an obligation to replace with a human institution that focused on natural rights and liberty. In effect, a hybrid "religion" flowed from the combination of Christian morality and Lockean liberal democratic theory. Although the form of government of a particular religious sect or denomination could be considered as dictated by God, the form of government for a civil society, consisting of many religious sects in addition to many non-religious peoples, was man made and left to the determination of the community's citizens, presumed to be educated in and responsible for their choices.

The biblical covenant was effectively merged with Locke's social contract. The biblical covenant was with God; the social contract was with the people.

Although the bible was not specifically used in support of rebellion, liberty, republican government, and separation of powers, Christians found many parallels in the bible to justify the end goals of separation from ruling authority, creation of a government where the people are the supreme power, and establishment of a governmental structure recognizing the depravity of man and the need to create a system of checks and balances within the governmental structure to counter man's depravity. As Christian evangelical minds and Enlightenment rational minds converged, the stage was set for the American Declaration of Independence and the Constitution to emerge and create a government where the people, rather than a ruling class, were the supreme power.

Christianity does not justify America's political contract and structure, nor does America's political contract and structure justify a Christian theocracy overlay to the government. Yet clearly, the Founding Fathers recognized the necessity of government to support religious education, from which students would learn the morals, ethics, character, and civic virtue considered necessary for the functioning of a government dedicated to securing the freedom and the common good of its citizens.

Chapter 2
On the Origins and Objectives of Progressivism and Liberal Progressivism

Late 19th Century and Early 20th Century Origins

About 100 years after adoption of the Constitution, the cultural foundations of unalienable natural rights, limited government, federalism, and consent of the governed came under attack as the size and complexity of America expanded. The Industrial Revolution clashed with America's rural roots, belief and faith in God clashed with the Enlightenment's faith in human reason and science alone. Intellectuals decided that man is perfectible, that intellectuals are more capable of knowing and implementing what is good for society than is the common man. The intellectual drivers of the Progressive movement in the United States focused less on the positive outcomes of America's Founding Principles and more on the negative outcomes of inequality of income, social status, and wealth. Rather than address the most egregious negative outcomes, Progressives then and now assume that America's Founding Principles were no longer appropriate and must be changed.

The concept of a government "of the people, by the people, and for the people," as proclaimed by Abraham Lincoln, was questioned by some influential intellectuals, one of whom, Woodrow Wilson, became the 28th President of the United States. During Wilson's term, several significant Progressive Amendments to the Constitution were adopted. Since then, incremental Progressive changes to America's Constitution and to America's social structure have been implemented, driving a wedge in the Union that has increasingly widened, especially since the mid-1960s. Unlike the wedge of slavery that divided the Southern slave states and the abolitionist Northern states, the current wedge is less visible on the surface. It pits Christians against secularists, Constitutional conservatives against Living Constitution progressives, haves against have-nots, limited "general welfare" proponents against broad-ranging "general welfare" proponents, capitalists against statists, among others. Both social and economic civil warfare sharply divide right from left; fortunately, the civil warfare remains uniquely American, fought not with guns but with legal briefs.

Some of the early proponents of Progressivism and the content of their speeches/writings included:

Woodrow Wilson, *The Study of Administration*, 1886 (It is only through independent regulatory agencies that government can pursue its necessary ends; government must make itself master of masterful corporations; calls for a new "science" – political science and the science of administration – looking to France and Germany where it is becoming highly developed;

administration [regulatory agencies charged with the development and implementation of civic policies and programs determined by scientific expertise] must be separated from politics [representation of the will of the people] and from the legislature; highly educated experts have technical expertise that political legislators do not; we try to do too much by the vote)

Woodrow Wilson, *Socialism and Democracy*, 1887 (Inherent natural rights rejected in favor of the idea that rights are a positive grant from government; limitation of public authority rejected for "state socialism;" public interests trump individual interests; omnipotence of legislation is the first postulate of all just political theory; the state may cross, at will, the line between private and public affairs; socialism and democracy are almost if not quite one and the same; men as communities are supreme over men as individuals; the concept of individual rights is an undemocratic radical political philosophy.)

Woodrow Wilson, *The Authors and Signers of the Declaration of Independence*, 1907 (Liberty is not absolute, but relative to its times; successful businesses must have obtained ill-gotten wealth and should be constrained and controlled by the federal government; morals are relative to the times and laws must be changed to reflect changing morals; but he recognizes that too

much regulation ultimately leads to socialism
and state ownership; he calls for individual
corporate leaders, not just their corporations, to
be held accountable for corporate law-breaking)

Woodrow Wilson, *The President of the United States*,
1908 (Constitutional checks and balances and
the separation of powers are indicative of the
flawed thinking of America's Founders;
government alone can provide the people's
needs; only the President represents the people
as a whole, yet he has limited power)

Woodrow Wilson, *Address to the Jefferson Club of Los
Angeles*, 1911 (Advised citizens to ignore the
heart of the Declaration of Independence, the
Preamble; big business castigated as controlling
politics and as have gotten wealth illegally;
majority tyranny proposed as superior to
minority tyranny, rather than rejection of both
types of tyranny)

Woodrow Wilson, *What is Progress*, 1913 (Big business
castigated;1787 Constitution depicted as
Newtonian and a "living" Constitution proposed
as a superior Darwinian model; checks and
balances of the 1787 Constitution depicted as too
constraining to Executive Power)

Woodrow Wilson, *The Old Order Changeth*, 1913
(Castigation of big business as a heartless system
of monopolies that control government; a call for
laws to protect the weak from the strong; life is

now so complicated compared to Jefferson's time that more laws and larger government are necessary; a call for radical and extended reconstruction of economic and political society)

Herbert Croly, *Progressive Democracy*, 1915 (Croly rejects the idea that government exists to protect individual rights; pure democracy, rather than the representative democracy of a Republic, is now possible because mass communication now makes it possible to know the people's desires quickly; a negative individualistic social policy implies a weak and irresponsible government whereas a positive comprehensive social policy implies a strong, efficient and responsible government.)

Frank Goodnow, *The American Conception of Liberty*, 1916 (Collective rights of society trump individual rights; legal contract rights granted by the society trump unalienable natural rights from the Creator)

Our Founders knew that a Constitutional Republic with separation of powers and the checks and balances of three branches of government would be a slow, somewhat messy, frustrating, and inefficient way to govern. The intellectuals who promoted Progressivism were frustrated with those features at the core of the American Constitutional Republic. They sought greater concentration of power in the Executive through the development of regulatory agencies with "expert scientific" staffing of those agencies and with legislative, executive, and judicial powers concentrated in the agencies. The powers of those agencies became greater and independent of the elected legislators and the judiciary.

Progressives recognized that slavery could not be eliminated by the Republic even half a century after the Constitution was written without a Civil War that took the lives of about 2% of the population at the time. Their observations about the political process and its participants convinced them that politics must be separated from the scientific administration of the government. They put their faith in a professional civil service staffed by experts in the various disciplines, because they believed that politicians had little expert knowledge, particularly as society and business had become far more complex than in the agrarian society of the late 18th century. They proposed and implemented regulatory agencies in the manner of German and other European governments, which they considered "best practice" models of governance. Whereas America's Founders sought to throw off the methods of the countries they left, America's new Progressive visionaries sought to copy those European methods. Today, one hundred years later, everyone can easily observe that the European Progressive approach to governing has failed to create a single global political, financial, business, and military power equal to the Constitutional Republic of the United States. Clearly, failure to fully embrace the European scientific administrative state approach to governing has enabled the United States to become and remain the world's beacon of hope, even to many in Progressive European societies.

The new Progressives rejected the Founders' concept of unalienable natural rights from a Creator in favor of positive rights granted by government. They rejected the Founders' insistence on the primacy of individual rights in favor of individual rights subordinate to collective rights of the community. They saw wisdom in the works of Hegel, Nietzsche, Marx, and Darwin, among others, during the time of great industrial progress in America, when the industrial revolution combined with individual freedom created great industrial corporations and wealthy industrialists. While industrial growth did create labor strife with working conditions & compensation, rather than focus solutions on resolving those particular issues, the new American Progressives joined in the global socialist and communist attacks on capitalism and private property ownership. They promoted the idea that such extraordinary wealth must have been obtained illegally and through oppressive working conditions for the laborers. A large part of the focus of the Progressives was on containment of large monopoly businesses and their owners, leading them to conclude that the Constitution devised by American's Founders was appropriate for the rural society of the 18th Century but that something new was required for the urban, industrial society of the late 19th and early 20th Centuries.

The Progressive ideology began evolving into a rejection of the Judeo Christian ethical values of absolute moral standards and proposed that morality is relative to the times and to the morality changes that occur in society. In other words, moral standards must follow societal changes rather than lead societal changes.

The core principles of Life, Liberty, and the Pursuit of Happiness contained in the Preamble of the Declaration of Independence were tossed aside as not central to the Declaration. Citizens were advised to focus instead on the list of the King's "injuries and usurpations," and create a new list of "injuries and usurpations" on a continuing basis over time, which they called a "living Constitution." The concept of a "fixed" Constitution was rejected and continues to be rejected ever more enthusiastically in the 21st Century.

Whereas the Founders feared tyrannies of a majority and of a minority, and devised the Constitutional Republic to repulse both types of tyrannies, and to protect the rights of the minority, the new Progressives believe in a Pure Democracy, which can easily result in tyranny of the majority. They came to believe in social justice rather than equal justice for rich and poor. Rather than churches, social organizations, and other private organizations caring for the poor and disadvantaged of American's society, they believed that government should become the primary provider of social welfare, with funds for doing so provided by taxes collected on the "illegally gotten profits" of the wealthy.

The early Progressives remained a religious people, still largely Christian, and made no significant attacks on the Christian values and principles that underlie America's Constitutional Republic. The attacks on the "separation of church and state" came later in the mid-20th Century.

Hallmark Progressive legislation was adopted with the passage of the 16th Amendment (Income Taxation) and the 17th Amendment (direct election of Senators), along with the 18th Amendment (Prohibition) which was later repealed by the 21st

Amendment. The 19th Amendment (Voting Rights for Women) was another major Progressive legislation. The 16th Amendment provided access to funds to pay for Progressive social programs, the 17th Amendment effectively neutered States rights by making the Senate responsive to the people rather than to the States. Both those Amendments allowed the Progressive ideology to grow stronger over the remainder of the 20th Century. The 19th Amendment righted a wrong much like the 15th Amendment did 50 years earlier.

During the 1920s, Progressivism had a brief respite, especially during the administration of Calvin Coolidge, who attempted to stall the growth of Progressive government's drive towards unlimited executive powers and unlimited growth of regulatory agencies. The Great Depression created an economic crisis of enormous proportions that unleashed the second phase of Progressivism, which took a giant leap forward during the administration of FDR. As a more recent 21st Century Progressive has stated, it represented an opportunity to "not let a crisis go to waste."

Chapter 2

The Second Great Wave of Progressive Attacks on Individual Liberty

Some of the most significant speeches and writings of the Great Depression era of Progressive growth and the content of those speeches and writings included the following.

> FDR, *Commonwealth Club Address*, 1932 (The Industrial Revolution changed the Founders' model with the rewards going to a few rather than to the many; with unequal outcomes, opportunity must also have been unequal; 600 corporations controlled 2/3 of American industry, while 10 million small businesses divided the remaining 1/3; economic oligarchy was the inevitable outcome; distributing wealth and products more equitably is the new task of government; the day of enlightened administration has arrived; uniform prosperity is the new task of government; restriction of the financier is necessary to protect individualism; the heads of finance and industry must sacrifice private advantage to achieve a common end.)

> John Dewey, *Liberalism and Social Action*, 1935 (Adopted Hegel's central themes of the denial of objective truth and the embracing of moral relativism; critical of the American founding, John Locke, and primacy of the individual over the state; positive law supreme over natural law; reinterpreted more broadly the "Public Welfare"

clause of the Constitution; equality of outcomes through social justice legislation stressed rather than equality of opportunity; sanctity of private property rejected; industry & finance socially directed by government to achieve organized social order rather than personal, individual liberty.)

FDR, *Democratic Convention Address*, 1936 (FDR's opponents of his programs are tagged as "economic royalists;" political tyranny of the 18th century has been replaced by economic tyranny of the 20th century, creating a new despotism, an industrial dictatorship; political inequality has been replaced by economic inequality; economic slavery has replaced racial slavery; government is to be remade into the very embodiment of human charity.)

FDR, *Annual Message to Congress*, 1944 (FDR's proposal for a "Second Bill of Rights," the last of which was implemented with Obamacare; political rights proved inadequate to assure us equality in the pursuit of happiness; true individual freedom cannot exist without economic security and independence; "Necessitous men are not free men;" "all of these rights spell security;" the grave dangers of "rightist reaction" shall have yielded to the spirit of Fascism if we should return to the "normalcy" of the 1920s.)

Much like the campaign of 2008, the Progressive rhetoric of the FDR campaign in 1932 reflected back upon an earlier period, in that case 30 years earlier to the late 19th century and early 20th century Industrial Revolution and the unequal distributions of wealth that occurred at that time. Rather than focus on the immediate causes and remedies of the Great Depression, the FDR campaign blamed big business, finance, "robber barons," among others for the crisis. Progressives used that opportunity to reprogram into the minds of the new generation the idealism of Progressive Utopian ideology, such as more equitable distribution of financial outcomes, the evils of big business and its leadership, enlightened expert scientific administration of government, and restraint of financiers and others who "surely caused" the Great Depression. Economic tyranny, rather than political tyranny, was the focus of the Progressive ideological messages of the 1930s.

This, combined with the Progressive reinterpretation of the Constitution's "general welfare clause," at the time of the Great Depression, ultimately led to the creation of a plethora of programs to secure "rights" beyond those of life, liberty, and the pursuit of happiness stated in the Declaration of Independence and guaranteed by the Constitution. A number of federal "work" programs were created during the Depression, the FHA was created to safeguard home ownership, and most importantly, the Social Security Administration was created to assure workers a minimum level of income during retirement. Greater equality of outcome rather than equality of opportunity was moved forward during the FDR years and the "collective good" rather than individual liberty was stressed.

In the State of the Union address of 1944, while the thoughts of the nation were focused on WWII and the coming invasion of Continental Europe, FDR proposed to Congress a major step in Progressive ideology. His Second Bill of Rights received scant attention among the general population, but Progressive politicians used it as the Operation Plan for the subsequent half century. Each element of FDR's Second Bill of Rights was implemented slowly, in small increments, hardly noticeable by citizens deeply engaged in the economic resurgence after WWII. By the time of the election of Barack Obama in 2008, all the major programs in FDR's Second Bill of Rights had been largely implemented except for nationalized health care. With the passage of Obamacare, all of FDR's Second Bill of Rights had now become law. Individual security for all rather than individual opportunity was the hallmark of FDR's Second Bill of Rights.

Chapter 2

The Emergence and Strengthening of *Liberal* Progressivism

After FDR, as the nation emerged from WWII as the world's greatest economic and military superpower, Progressivism's growth was slow until the mid-1960s, a time of great social upheaval, an unpopular war, and rebellion of youth against the moral and ethical principles and values of prior generations. This period of time enabled the next "great leap" in Progressivism, which was far more radical than the two prior "great leaps." Prior to the 1960s, Progressives generally held the same moral, spiritual, and ethical principles and values of the founders, anchored by Judeo Christian morality. American were still largely church-attending Christians and the traditional family was revered by politicians and citizens alike. That changed with the turbulent 60's.

Some of the most significant speeches and writings by Progressive thinkers and leaders from that time until the current period, and the content of those speeches and writings, include the following.

> LBJ, *Remarks at the University of Michigan Commencement*, 1964 (LBJ's call for A Great Society; abundance and liberty for all.)

> LBJ, *The Nationwide War on the Sources of Poverty*, 1964 (Remarks to Congress on the submission of the Economic Opportunity Act of 1964; the Act provides several basic "opportunities" including establishment of the Office of Economic Opportunity, a Job Corps, a Community Action

Program; appeals to the "general welfare" clause of the Constitution as the basis for social welfare programs and to extend that welfare to all our people as a right to ensure greater equality of outcomes.)

LBJ, *Remarks Upon Accepting the Nomination*, 1964 (Generally a restatement of FDR's Second Bill of Rights; "for more than 30 years, from social security to the war against poverty, we have diligently worked to enlarge the freedom of man;" generally equating equality of outcomes with freedom.)

LBJ, *Toward Full Educational Opportunity*, 1965 (State of the Union address; references the declaration in the Northwest Ordinance of 1787 that "schools and the means of education shall forever be encouraged;" but uses the declaration as a means to extend greater federal direction over what has historically been a local matter - education.)

LBJ, *Commencement Address at Howard University*, 1965 ("Not just equality of opportunity, but equality as a result;" justice is to fulfill the fair expectations of man.)

Justice William Brennan, *Speech at the Text and Teaching Symposium*, 1985 (Electorally unaccountable Justices with the power to invalidate the expressed desires of representative bodies on the ground of inconsistency with higher law in fidelity to "the intentions of the Framers" is little more than arrogance cloaked as humility; the ultimate question must be, what do the words of the text mean in our time; what this text is about is the relationship of the individual and the state; the possibilities for collision between government activity and individual rights will increase as the power and authority of government itself expands; recognition of so-called "new property rights" in those receiving government entitlements affirms the essential dignity of the least fortunate among us by demanding that government treat with decency, integrity and consistency those dependent on its benefits for their very survival.)

Peter Orszag, *Too Much of a Good Thing: Why We Need Less Democracy*, 2011 (Call to counter legislative gridlock by making government less democratic by jettisoning the pure representative democracy of a Republic; automatic stabilizers proposed, such as progressive taxation, unemployment insurance, and others that take effect without action of Congress and that require Congress to say "no" rather than to say "yes;" government would be less accountable to voters.)

Sanford Levinson, *Our Imbecilic Constitution*, 2012 (Call for elimination of the Electoral College and of the equality of vote in the Senate of small and large states; call for elimination of "checks and balances" and "separation of powers;" call for greater ease in amending the Constitution; call for enhanced power in the office of the President by giving him the ability to appoint a specific number to the House and Senate to do his will more easily.)

Civil rights for blacks took center stage in the late 1950s, followed by the Vietnam War in the 1960s. The social upheaval brought about by these two major events masked a major increase in Progressivism that began in the same period. It proved to be relatively easy for the Johnson Administration and Congress to pass Progressive legislation in the 1960s because Democrats held majorities in both houses of Congress as well as the Presidency.

LBJ's Great Society initiative and the War on Poverty were the major Progressive initiatives, significant steps in implementing FDR's Second Bill of Rights, moving increasingly towards greater equality of outcomes for all Americans. Reinterpretation of the "general welfare" and the "necessary and proper" clauses of the Constitution enabled Progressives to move the needle farther to the left. Even the 1787 Northwest Ordinance was invoked to expand educational funding and opportunities to more Americans – ironic that Progressives would use a 1787 law to support their agenda at the same time they began to assault the 1787 Constitution as no longer applicable to modern America.

At the same time, the attack on Christianity began. Thomas Jefferson had written a letter to Baptists in Connecticut, where the state-supported denomination was not Baptist, assuring them that federal law would not infringe upon their right to worship. Progressives reinterpreted this single phrase to mean that religion must be removed from the public square and from public education. This attack has continued to the current day with hardly anyone bothering to determine the context of what Jefferson might have meant when he wrote about a "wall of separation between church and state."

The sexual revolution and drug experimentation also began in the 1960s. The combination of the attacks on Christianity, the loosening of sexual standards, increased drug experimentation, and the relaxation of divorce requirements led to a slow moving decline in moral, religious, and traditional family values.

Progressivism had taken on a new face, moving the needle ever more to the left, repudiating the Constitutional Republic established by our Founding Fathers and renewing the "economic inequalities" argument that was the focus of the Wilson and FDR presidencies. It sought to replace the moral and ethical principles of Christianity with moral relativism, and equality of opportunity with equality of outcome. Multiculturalism and post-modernism grew over the decades since the 1960s. Postmodernism is an attempt to fundamentally transform American society and culture. The new era of *Liberal* Progressivism (LiPro) had begun.

Increasingly the Courts were used by LiPros to "legislate" abortion for all, removal of prayer in the schools, and in 2015 the redefinition of marriage. Executive departments under the President were expanded to increase the power of the executive and reduce the legislative power of

Congress. Entitlement benefits were expanded to cover an increasing percentage of Americans, ultimately leading to an unsustainably large increase in the national debt.

Limited government had been replaced by unlimited government. Calls for a "living Constitution," for elimination of the checks and balances among the three branches of government and for the elimination of the separation of powers established by our Founding Fathers have become increasingly strong as Liberal Progressivism has been sold as the means to an earthly Utopia for all.

Chapter 3
On the Present State of the American Experiment

It was the Colonies' intellectual elites who led the Colonies to revolution and who designed the Constitutional Republic in the 18th century. Many lived primarily in urban regions of the colonies and were heavily influenced by Enlightenment rational thought, tempering biblical revelation with human reason. But they understood the necessity of Judeo Christian education for all citizens and acceptance of rational Judeo Christian values and principles as necessary for the success of the traditional liberal democratic government they created.

Since the creation of the Republic, particularly since the late 19th century and early 20th century, America's intellectual elites have continued to lead the American Constitutional Republic, but often in a direction different from that of America's Founding Fathers. This should not be surprising since America, over the past two hundred years, has become increasingly more urban with each generation attaining ever higher levels of education. Today's intellectual elites overwhelmingly occupy America's educational institutions, particularly universities and colleges of education, giving them ever greater opportunities to influence the thinking of students attending those schools, and particularly future teachers. At the same time, religious education and religious educators have declined sharply, and the cost of attending religious schools has increased to a level making such schools unaffordable to many who might prefer to attend those institutions.

Before the middle of the 20th century, most political intellectual elites leading America in this direction continued to support traditional family values and Judeo Christian morality and ethical principles. Since the middle of the 20th century, attacks on the traditional American, Judeo Christian, and liberal-democratic Republic have dramatically changed America. Christianity, in particular, has been denigrated in favor of a completely secular nation; the traditional family has been denigrated in favor of all varieties of family; equality of opportunity has been denigrated in favor of equality of outcome; and limited government has been denigrated in favor of expanded government. Americans financially dependent primarily on government have increased to a point where that number may already exceed those who are not totally or partially financially dependent on government.

Chapter Four, *Tyranny Is Tyranny*, of Howard Zinn's "*A People's History of the United States*," discusses the period leading up to the Declaration of Independence. The general theme of the chapter is that the objective of the Founding Fathers was to rid themselves of the ruling Aristocracy of Britain and replace it with a new aristocracy of rich and powerful white male owners of property in the Colonies. In line with the title of the chapter, one source of tyranny would be replaced by another source of tyranny, with the new powerful elite being local rather than in a country far distant. The poor, women, slaves, and wage earners would experience no change in their status, with the same inequalities in wealth and income remaining after the Declaration of Independence as were in existence before the Declaration.

Zinn's research discovered sufficient numbers of people and quotations to support the theme of the chapter and, presumably, the consistent theme of the entire book. Locke and his "*Second Treatise on Government,*" Adam Smith and his "*The Wealth of Nations,*" and Thomas Paine and his "*Common Sense,*" are dismissed as tools for the preservation of the economic inequality of the Colonies after ridding the nation of British economic repression. The wealthy and propertied of the Colonies are presumed to have used whatever tools they could gather to present the appearance of a unified populace in support of the revolution. Unifying the populace required convincing the underclasses that their support of a revolution would result in economic and social liberty after the revolution. Zinn posited that the reality was that the wealthy leaders of the revolution needed the underclasses only as soldiers in the militia to do the fighting and dying so that the wealthy could establish their own tyrannical rule over them when independence was achieved.

Zinn dismisses Jefferson's sincerity in his drafting of the Preamble to the Declaration of Independence because of Jefferson's ownership of slaves then and until his death in 1826. He overlooks the many written and spoken comments of Jefferson in which Jefferson clearly stated his desire for slavery to be abolished and Zinn even dismisses the paragraph on the abolition of slavery in Jefferson's draft of the Declaration as disingenuous because Jefferson would have known that the Continental Congress would eliminate the paragraph from the final approved Declaration.

No doubt the arguments against income and wealth disparity, as well as the arguments against class, race, and gender disparities, existed in the 18th century as well as they exist today and as they have existed throughout all of written history. These same arguments are eternal and will exist until the end of the human race on earth. It is well that we humans be reminded of our need to be cognizant of the less fortunate in society and that those who have wealth and power be reminded of their duty to use their wealth and power responsibly and that justice be applied uniformly without regard to these differences. Judeo Christian biblical passages clearly articulate these principles.

However, influential Progressive communicators like Zinn, continue to rail against America, America's Founding Fathers, America's Founding documents, and America's Constitutional Republic. They do so more than 200 years after America's founding, even after observing the disastrous effects of 19th Century Socialist and Marxist philosophies on societies and countries that have adopted those philosophies focused on equality of outcome, wealth redistribution, and statism. Tens of millions, if not hundreds of millions, of people have died at the hands of national leaders who have attempted to implement these philosophies during the 20th century. Historical revisionists like Zinn ignore the failing of many such continuing experiments as they write their "histories." They ignore the failing experiments in Cuba, China, Venezuela, Muslim theocracies, among others, as they condemn America's highly successful experiment.

While those redistributive philosophies were being implemented elsewhere, America's 18th century experiment has proven that its version of a Republic, focused on rule of law, limited government, individual liberty, equality of opportunity rather than equality of outcome, and equal justice rather than social justice has achieved a far greater breadth of wealth, income, and freedom across all social classes than any other country over the course of the past 200 years. Why proponents of other philosophies choose to focus on the minimal negatives of America's Republican experiment rather than on the enormous positives is a psychological mystery. America has so many positive attributes to celebrate and to encourage its citizens to aspire to even higher levels of achievement; spending so much time focusing on the negatives only encourages behavior that frustrates America's continued growth and takes everyone's eyes off America's positive potential for the future.

The economic divide is real, not only in America but in all nations of the world, free and not free, democratic and authoritarian. In America, even those on the lowest economic ladder have much compared to middle class citizens in most nations of the world. Yet, the income and wealth disparity is used no longer by the champions of those on the lower economic levels to provide economic hope to those aspiring to rise; rather, they seek to lower the economic rewards to those who have achieved economic success in the name of collective prosperity. But the march towards collective prosperity most frequently results in collective poverty.

At the same time, some business leaders who have achieved economic success may appear more interested in accumulating even greater personal wealth and income than in sharing some of the increase in the profit pie with employees who helped generate the larger pie. Equality of outcome should not be the goal however. What has made America great has been individual freedom to pursue happiness, including economic happiness; until recently, collective happiness has never trumped personal happiness. When an individual achieves his economic happiness, he then has always been free to share his property with others, as encouraged by his Judeo Christian morality and ethics to serve his fellow man. When those rational Judeo Christian ethics and moralities are absent, self-centeredness is more likely to follow. So, it is more important now than ever for America's people to recommit to religious faith with morality and ethics consistent with Judeo Christian morality and ethics.

A major factor in the economic-divide warfare can be traced directly to the increasing divide in social factors, particularly the erosion of Judeo Christian values and principles and the adoption of secular relative values. Strong Judeo Christian values and principles would help those on the lower economic levels reject economic envy and also help those on the upper economic levels be more willing to more generously share their economic success with those on the lower economic levels of American society. Unless this trend towards increased secularism can be reversed, it is unlikely that the economic divide battle will resolve itself amicably. A purely secular law-based commandment to redistribute property to others can never substitute for a heart-felt desire to aid those less fortunate, based on shared values and principles accepted by faith and a willingness to please God, rather than a commandment to comply with secular legal codes.

The Founding Fathers encouraged education in general and specifically education in religion to enable citizens to acquire moral and ethical mindsets that would lead to civic virtue. Civic virtue cannot evolve from the independent minds of 300 million citizens and be codified into laws and regulations that all, or even a substantial portion, of 300 million people would believe to be reasonable. Shared moral and ethical mindsets are developed by reference to religious moral codes of conduct that set a higher standard than most people would set on their own. Left to devise their own standards, the natural self-centeredness of human beings will provide lower standards for themselves and higher standards for all others, with no set of shared values and principles.

Yet the prevailing trend over many generations has been the secularization of America, the supposition that religion has no role in our society or government. Rather, proponents of a purely secular America state that religion is only a personal choice, not related to morality, ethics, or civic virtue. As such, it is to be eliminated from public life and practiced in solitude or with other like-minded humans in private venues, not on government property, in governmental institutions, or in public schools. The proponents of this philosophy wrongly assume that *any* public display of religious philosophies, objects, or documents is an attempt to create a theocracy.

Today's Liberal Progressives proclaim that all values and principles are equal, that no set of such values and principles trumps any other set, and that all values are relative and none are absolute. Our Founding Fathers would, and did, strongly disagree. A society and culture with no absolute values is a society in decline.

Today's Liberal Progressives proclaim that social issues are off the table for discussion in political campaigns and that economic issues are the primary political issues. The environment, bigotry, class contempt, social sins, climate change, the earth, and animals are the primary non-economic concerns of Liberal Progressives.

The focus of Progressives and Liberal Progressives on equality of outcomes has proven difficult to achieve under the structure of government established more than 200 years ago by our Founding Fathers. They want a new "living Constitution" to replace our current Constitution to enable them to legislate equality of outcomes through redistribution. Liberal Progressives have achieved enormous success in populating America's education establishments, from preschool through university, allowing them to craft messages delivered to students that reflect Liberal Progressive philosophy. Changing the "corporate culture" of the Constitutional Republic, with its focus on a federal government designed to have limited powers and encumbered by checks and balances to avoid concentration of power in any one branch of government, has proven to be a far more formidable task than Progressives hoped. However, they have been opportunistic by "never letting a crisis go to waste."

Over more than 100 years, Progressives have succeeded in growing government, widening its breadth and power over the individual. They have used periods of economic and social disruption to establish government programs and agencies that use tax dollars to do far more than pay the operational expenses of government. Far more tax dollars now are transferred from one group of citizens to another group of citizens than are used for essential government operations. The term "mandatory spending" in a government generally means spending for the operational expenses of government and "discretionary spending" means spending for social welfare programs. But today's federal budget classifies mandatory spending to include primarily transfer payments of tax dollars from one group of citizens to another group and discretionary spending to include what common sense reasoning would classify as mandatory (e.g., defense, infrastructure, foreign relations).

Liberal Progressives also have argued, and continue to argue, for a "Living Constitution," a new Constitution that eliminates the checks and balances our Founding Fathers so wisely incorporated in the Constitution under which America has thrived for more than 200 years. As James Madison, primary author of the Constitution, noted in *Federalist 51*, "If men were angels, no government would be necessary. If angels were to govern men, neither external nor internal controls on government would be necessary." The nature of man has not changed over the past quarter millennial; there is no less need for checks and balances today than there was in the late 18th century. Yet the Progressive attacks on America's Constitutional Republican structure of government continue.

Almost 50% of America's citizens today receive part or all of their income from the federal government; approximately 15% receive food stamps to buy their food; now the 15 to 20% of American business that provides health care services is essentially controlled by the federal government. Liberal Progressives have exploited the Executive branch of government by legally creating a labyrinth of federal agencies with legislative, executive, and judicial powers concentrated within the agencies to exert control over the remaining 80 to 85% of American business. The growth of these federal agencies plows a path leading to economic fascism, where individuals are permitted to own businesses, but have little power to conduct their business in ways that they deem most efficient and effective. The consequence is that, although the Constitution remains intact, with no "living Constitution" having replaced it, the exploitation of the Executive Branch's powers to create regulatory agencies with concentration of powers has to a large extent been effective in restricting the individual freedom our Founding Fathers fought so hard to achieve. The limited government design embedded into our Constitution has eroded substantially, especially over the past one hundred years; the scope and power of government has become increasingly unrestricted.

Now is the time to celebrate how America achieved its global lead in social and economic liberty and redirect our country and people back to that course of success.

Chapter 4

On the Need to Rejuvenate the American Experiment

In 1782, the Great Seal of the United States of America was approved; each of the elements on the Seal's two sides communicates to future generations the important principles and values the Founding Fathers wished to pass on. On the reverse side is an Eye of Providence (Providence was the term used in that era to signify the Judeo/Christian God's ongoing presence guiding the affairs of men) and the Latin words *Annuit Coeptis*, meaning *He Favors our Undertakings*. Clearly, our Founding Fathers desired to pass on to future generations the importance of faith not only in our nation's founding, but for the entire future life of the Republic they founded. God's providence meant then, and means today, that God is active in our lives and in the life of our country, and not merely an idle bystander who created the world and then abandoned it. Our Founding Fathers intended for Americans to live by, and guide America by, the core principles of the Judeo/Christian faith that "all good men could agree upon."

John Adams said that if a nation would "take the Bible for their only law book, and every member should regulate his conduct by the precepts there exhibited, what a Utopia, a Paradise would this region be." He was not speaking about

55

only the divine revelation of the Bible as believed by orthodox Christians, but of those principles and codes of conduct found throughout the Old and New Testaments upon which, as Franklin said "all good men could agree."

Adams, and the other Founding Fathers, believed that "our Constitution was made only for a moral land of religious people; it is wholly inadequate to the government of any other." Jefferson said that the teachings of Jesus contained "the most sublime and benevolent code of morals which has ever been offered to man." And Franklin believed that religious morality made good citizens, good citizens promoted public morality, and public morality benefited society. Even Gouverneur Morris, whose personal immorality was widely known, said "destruction of religion loosened the bonds of duty; and those of allegiance must ever be weak, where there is a defect both of piety and morality; and religion is the only solid basis of morals, and morals are the only possible support of free governments."

Even orthodox Christians, who believe that man is fallen and sinful and in constant need of repentance, God's mercy and grace, acknowledge that the ideal and high standard of biblical morality is unreachable and that human law is necessary unless one lives alone on an island. But, Adams is correct. The Judeo/Christian Bible has provided the best idealistic standards available to Americans since our nation's founding. Rather than dismiss that excellent resource, our current political leaders should do as our Founding Fathers did and encourage Americans to know, understand, and apply the moral and ethical principles found in the Judeo/Christian bible. That alone may be insufficient for true Christian fellowship, but it can be sufficient for civic fellowship in a complex and religiously diverse civil society in which freedom of religious belief and thought are the essence of civic rights.

Some examples include the following. Franklin's "all good men could agree" with most of the 10 Commandments from Exodus 20, specifically honor your mother and father, don't murder, don't commit adultery, don't steal, don't give false testimony, and don't envy what others have. All could also agree with the eight Beatitudes of Matthew 5. 1 Corinthians 13 presents the characteristics of love that no one could disagree with. The Fruit of the Spirit of Galatians 5 (love, joy, peace, patience, kindness, goodness, faithfulness, gentleness and self-control) should be agreeable to everyone. And from the Armor of God of Ephesians 6, no objections are likely to two of the six characteristics listed, the belt of truth and the breastplate of righteousness.

Apologists for various sides of the discussions about the religious foundation and character of America and the beliefs of our Founding Fathers spend virtually all of their time and energy arguing about which Founding Fathers were orthodox Christian, Deist, Unitarian, and agnostic. They will never agree on this. Their time would be better invested in cooperation to compile the core characteristics, as noted above, upon which all of our Founding Fathers did agree and to incorporate those characteristics into a coherent civic spiritual political philosophy upon which our great nation was built and which can and should continue to guide America over the next 200 years.

Moral and ethical principles found in the texts of other religions can likewise be held up as core principles; more likely than not, many of the principles are likely to overlap with those of the Judeo Christian Bible. A commandment to murder "infidels" would be in conflict with the Judeo Christian codes, along with many other religious groups' codes, with no demonstration of love of and service to others, and would be rejected. The American military also has strong moral and ethical principles worthy of incorporation into America's code of morality and ethics. For example, West Point's Honor Code simply states "A cadet will not lie, cheat, steal, or tolerate those who do."

Orthodox Christians believe that there is only one path to God, that path being orthodox Christianity. It is perfectly understandable that orthodox Christians should want to show others that path. And it is perfectly permissible, under the provisions of the 1st Amendment, for orthodox Christians, as well as members of other faiths, to publicly proclaim and display their religious beliefs by praying in public, displaying and reading (during breaks and meal times) a Holy Book in their place of work (even in government offices and schools), among other acts common among members of their faith's belief system.

However, as employees, orthodox members of any religious faith should always understand that their employers and supervisors may not be amenable, in a diverse workplace, to some more open displays of faith, believing that such displays are disruptive to others of different beliefs in the workplace. They should also understand that they should not use the work place to convert others to their faith without permission of their employers. In the workplace, actions speak louder than words, books, and religious artifacts and those actions alone can influence a co-worker to want to meet after work to learn how to live a similar life.

Good morals, values, and ethical principles, leading to civic virtue, along with duty to love, serve, and respect others, were the focus of our Founding Fathers' Constitutional deliberations. Whatever a religious person believes, whether just core principles or denominational additions to the core principles, was acceptable to the founders provided that such beliefs had good consequences for society. If the consequences were not good for society, then those beliefs were not acceptable. Discussions of political hot potatoes, such as abortion and same-sex marriage, can be far more effective if they focus on discussions of core moral principles, natural law, and the effect on civic virtue rather than on Biblical sin and eternal damnation.

Rather than continue to press for a completely secular nation, politicians and political leaders should encourage religious faith for all citizens and not require that all expressions of faith be conducted only in the privacy of one's home or place of worship. Religious faith was one of the critical components of our nation's founding and success since founding. The future success of America and its standing as an island of civic virtue in a sea of turmoil and conflict, is lessened by continuing the drift towards a totally secular nation. We should work diligently to draw from sacred texts those moral and ethical principles and values towards which we Americans should be striving and encourage all citizens to better understand their faiths and be willing to discuss those principles that are important for civic virtue. The starting point can be love of neighbor and personal acts of charity for our neighbor. Our Constitutional Republic will not likely survive without a return to a vibrant and public faith.

Individual rights are the core of the Declaration of Independence, the Constitution, and the Bill of Rights. Our Founding Fathers believed that government's primary responsibility was to protect the unalienable rights of individuals, not to grant rights to individuals. The political arguments of the early 21st century are not new; they are evergreen. Citizens must be vigilant throughout their lives to observe and counter the arguments for fundamental change to our founding documents, our founding philosophy, and our founding morality and ethics. The incremental repression of individual rights in favor of collective rights and the Progressive drive to replace the Constitution has been addressed by many political leaders in the 20th century. Among those are the following:

Winston Churchill, *What's a Good Constitution* (1936), written during a period of deep global economic stress, is as current a commentary as could be written during the current period of major social & economic stress.

"In the United States, also, economic crisis has led to an extension of the activities of the Executive and to the pillorying, by irresponsible agitators, of certain groups and sections of the population as enemies of the rest. There have been efforts to exalt the power of the central government and to limit the rights of individuals. It has been sought to mobilize behind this reversal of the American tradition, at once the selfishness of the pensioners, or would-be pensioners, of Washington, and the patriotism of all who wish to see their country prosperous once more. Civilization means that officials and authorities, whether uniformed or not, whether armed or not, are made to realize that they are servants and not masters.

The onus must lie always upon those who propose a change, and the process of change is hardly ever beneficial unless it considers what is due to the past as well as what is claimed for the future. The question we are discussing is whether a fixed constitution is a bulwark or a fetter. From what I have written it is plain that I incline to the side of those who would regard it as a bulwark, and that I rank the citizen higher than the State, and regard the State as useful only in so far as it preserves his inherent rights. All forms of tyranny are odious. It makes very little difference to the citizen, father of a family, head of a household, whether tyranny comes from a royal or imperial despot, or from a Pope or Inquisitor, or from a military caste, or from an aristocratic or plutocratic oligarchy, or from a ring of employers, or a trade union, or a party caucus—or worst of all, from a terrified and infuriated mob.

It may well be that this very quality of rigidity, which is today thought to be so galling, has been a prime factor in founding the greatness of the United States. In the shelter of the Constitution nature has been conquered, a mighty continent has been brought under the sway of man, and an economic entity established, unrivalled in the whole history of the globe.

And here we must note a dangerous misuse of terminology. 'Taking the rigidity out of the American Constitution' means, and is intended to mean, new gigantic accessions of power to the dominating center of government and giving it the means to make new fundamental laws enforceable upon all American citizens. The so-called 'rigidity' of the American Constitution is in fact the guarantee of freedom to its widespread component parts. That a set of persons, however eminent, carried into office upon some populist heave, should have the power to make the will of a bare majority effective over the whole of the United States might cause disasters upon the greatest scale from which recovery would not be swift or easy. The rigidity of the Constitution of the United States is the shield of the common man."

Calvin Coolidge, *The Inspiration of the Declaration*, 1926, from his speech on the 150th anniversary of the Declaration, provides sufficient argument even today why a "living Constitution" is no more appropriate today than it was almost 100 years ago when the idea was already being proposed by early-20th century Progressives.

"It was not because it was proposed to establish a new nation, but because it was proposed to establish a nation on new principles, that July 4, 1776, has come to be regarded as one of the greatest days in history. Three very definite propositions were set out in its preamble regarding the nature of mankind and therefore of government. These were the doctrine that all men are created equal, that they are endowed with certain inalienable rights, and that therefore the source of the just powers of government must be derived from the consent of the governed. No one can examine this record and escape the conclusion that in the great outline of its principles the Declaration was the result of the religious teachings of the preceding period. They are found in the texts, the sermons, and the writings of the early colonial clergy who were earnestly undertaking to instruct their congregations in the great mystery of how to live.

It is often asserted that the world has made a great deal of progress since 1776, that we have had new thoughts and new experiences which have given us a great advance over the people of that day, and that we may therefore very well discard their conclusions for something more modern. But that reasoning cannot be applied to this great charter. If all men are created equal, that is final. If they are endowed with inalienable rights, that is final. If governments derive their just powers from the consent of the governed, that is final. No advance, no progress can be made beyond these propositions. If anyone wishes to deny their truth or their soundness, the only direction in which he can proceed historically is not forward, but backward toward the time when there was no equality, no rights of the individual, no rule of the people. Those who wish to proceed in that direction cannot lay claim to progress. They are reactionary. Their ideas are not more modern, but more ancient, than those of the Revolutionary fathers."

Ronald Reagan, *A Time for Choosing*, 1964, a speech delivered at a time of national angst and revolution. Legitimate protests against racial bigotry became violent protests. Civil rights legislation, the beginnings of an unpopular war, major advances in progressive policies to attack poverty by plowing enormous sums of money into a "War on Poverty" that, more than 50 years later is reported to require ever more good money after bad, move America deeper into a socialist Utopian experiment. Reagan's wisdom then is wholly applicable today.

We may not have explicitly chosen the Liberal Progressive path in the mid-60s, but we effectively chose that path by our failure to continue the fight begun in the 18th century because we allowed Liberal Progressives to define the agenda after the mid-60s.

Reagan said "It seems impossible to legitimately debate the issues of the day without being subjected to name-calling and the application of labels. Those who deplore use of the terms "pink" and "leftist" are themselves guilty of branding all who oppose their liberalism as right wing extremists.

It's time we asked ourselves if we still know the freedoms intended for us by the Founding Fathers. I suggest to you there is no left or right, only an up or down. Regardless of their humanitarian purpose, those who would sacrifice freedom for security have, whether they know it or not, chosen this downward path. Plutarch warned, 'The real destroyer of the liberties of the people is he who spreads among them bounties, donations, and benefits.'

The full power of centralized government was the very thing the Founding Fathers sought to minimize. They knew you don't control things; you can't control the economy without controlling *people*. So we have come to a time for choosing. Either we accept the responsibility for our own destiny, or we abandon the American Revolution and confess that an intellectual belief in a far-distant capitol can plan our lives for us better than we can plan them ourselves. It is in the area of social welfare that government has found its most fertile growing bed. So many of us accept our responsibility for those less fortunate. We are susceptible to humanitarian appeals.

Chapter 4

But any time we question the schemes of the do-gooders, we are denounced as being opposed to their humanitarian goal. It seems impossible to legitimately debate their solutions with the assumption that all of us share the desire to help those less fortunate. They tell us we are always against, never for anything. Well, it isn't so much that liberals are ignorant. It's just that they know so much that isn't so.

Because no government ever voluntarily reduces itself in size, government programs once launched never go out of existence. A government agency is the nearest thing to eternal life we'll ever see on this earth. Already we have a permanent structure so big and complex it is virtually beyond the control of Congress and the comprehension of the people, and tyranny inevitably follows when this permanent structure usurps the policy-making function that belongs to elected officials.

We approach a point of no return when government becomes so huge and entrenched that we fear the consequences of upheaval and just go along with it. If some among you fear taking a stand because you are afraid of reprisals from customers, clients, or even government, recognize that you are just feeding the crocodile hoping he'll eat you last.

Those who ask us to trade our freedom for the soup kitchen of the welfare state are architects of a policy of accommodation. They tell us that by avoiding a direct confrontation with the enemy he will learn to love us and give up his evil ways. All who oppose this idea are blanket indicted as warmongers.

You and I have a rendezvous with destiny. We can preserve for our children this, the last best hope of man on earth, or we can sentence them to take the first step into a thousand years of darkness. If we fail, at least let our children and our children's children say of us we justified our brief moment here. We did all that could be done."

Ronald Reagan, *First Inaugural Address* (1981), can be repeated by a Republican candidate in any current-day election.

"For decades, we have piled deficit upon deficit, mortgaging our future and our children's future for the temporary convenience of the present. To continue this long trend is to guarantee tremendous social, cultural, political, and economic upheavals.

From time to time, we have been tempted to believe that society has become too complex to be managed by self-rule, that government by an elite group is superior to government for, by, and of the people. But if no one among us is capable of governing himself, then who among us has the capacity to govern someone else?

It is no coincidence that our present troubles parallel and are proportionate to the intervention and intrusion in our lives that result from unnecessary and excessive growth of government. It is time to reawaken this industrial giant, to get government back within its means, and to lighten our punitive tax burden. And these will be our first priorities, and on these principles, there will be no compromise."

President Reagan's statement that "we have come to a time for choosing" is even more appropriate today than it was in 1964, or even in 1981. For most of the 20th century, we chose passively, by silence. Deciding not to choose is a decision to accept what someone else chooses for us. Many citizens continue to prefer to passively accept Liberal Progressive changes as they occur and express their displeasure after the choices are made for them. Passive choosing can lead down only one path. Whining about the choices made for us will not repeal those choices. Only active involvement can do so.

Active involvement, however, must be more than the relatively passive actions of writing to congress members, contributing money to politicians and their campaigns, and showing up at Tea Party rallies. Citizens must become "active" in the truest sense of the word.

The Baby Boom generation has fully enjoyed, from birth through today, the fruits of our great nation's economic and political success. The first of that generation reached the traditional retirement age of 65 in 2011; the last of that generation will do so in the year 2029. Each generation must hand off the cultural football to the generation following it. Over the decades since the birth of the first baby boomer, the football has become wet and slippery. We would be irresponsible to hand off a slippery football.

As the baby boom generation retires, its members have another choice. Some, especially those who have not managed to save sufficient assets, will find that they must continue to work. Their choices are limited.

Others have accumulated sufficient assets to enable them to leave the workforce entirely. Many will spend more time with children and grandchildren; they have an opportunity to dry the cultural football and pass it off to the next generations. That is necessary, but still not sufficient.

Many will choose to pursue pleasure, frivolity, and merriment masquerading as happiness, believing that they've "earned it" after many decades of work. "Earned" pleasure is deserved and should be enjoyed, but it too is necessary but still not sufficient.

Those who recognize that God owns all they have, and even those who don't believe that God owns all they have, but who believe that giving back is important, can easily understand the need to "actively" pass their wisdom on to more than just their own children and grandchildren.

All who can afford to "retire" and enjoy "earned pleasure" must accept responsibility to pass on the cultural heritage of the United States to more than just members of their own families.

Such "active" involvement can take many forms including, but not limited to, church youth groups, veterans' organizations activities involving youth, high-school ROTC programs, service organizations, and especially school volunteers. Attending school programs in which their children and grandchildren are involved is important and necessary, but serving school children not in one's family is critical, because so many other parents and grandparents are unable or unwilling to serve.

Rekindling the American Experiment requires much more than mere recognition of the problem and communication of the problem to others of like mind (i.e., speaking to the choir). If recognition and communication, combined with a fear that one's children and grandchildren will not be able to enjoy the lifestyle and economic rewards that we've enjoyed, are not accompanied by "action," then the American Experiment will die a slow and painful death. Many believe that this might occur within only one or two more generations.

So let us resolve that active "service above self" will be our mantra. Let us resolve that we will seek out opportunities to serve today's students from elementary school through college. Let us resolve that we will study our nation's culture, origins, founding documents, and Founding Fathers so we can intelligently communicate that knowledge along with our "personal testimony" to future generations.

To act upon those resolves will require some discipline, which may be difficult when one has finally achieved success. A simple discipline of committing one or two hours of service for every one hour of pleasure might work for some. For others, committing eight hours of service per week might work. The point is that a commitment will not be transformed into action unless the time is allocated and put into one's weekly calendar as consistently as one's weekly golf round, card game, or dining out.

The time for action has arrived. Our children's and grandchildren's generations need our knowledge and wisdom about those features of our nation's cultural heritage that have made the "great experiment" an economic, cultural, and political success and a magnet for people from all over the world.

In summary, let us not throw under the bus one of the other critical components of the success of America – the Constitution, with its focus on the protection of individual rights, separation of powers and system of checks and balances to avoid concentration of power in any one branch or person or agency of government. As Churchill said, "the rigidity of the Constitution is the shield of the common man."

A "Living Constitution" will weaken all that has made America the greatest success story in the annals of history. As Coolidge said, the core principles in the Declaration of Independence are "final." The ideas of modern Liberal Progressives are reactionary and regressive, not more modern.

This will require not only an increased emphasis on the education of our children and grandchildren about our national heritage and culture, but also an emphasis on the education of voting-age adults, who likely have merely accepted our government's structure without fully understanding why it is as it is and why it is important to retain and frequently revitalize it.

As Reagan noted more than 50 years ago, security purchased at the price of freedom is a vote for a downward path, for a destruction of true liberty. Making people's security depend on government enables government to control people; once the people are controlled, centralized control over all else comes easily.

Reagan stated then that we have reached a "time for choosing." We let that time pass, and by passively accepting small incremental Liberal Progressive changes since then, we've effectively chosen security over liberty. Although the window is closing, there remains time to choose; the question is, are the American people willing to choose liberty, or has the American "pursuit of happiness" been fully achieved with government-granted security rather than with individual opportunity?

The growth of government agencies that Reagan observed in the 1960s has progressed at a rate that would not surprise Reagan, given our passive acceptance of gifts from Washington under the umbrella of security. We must press our politicians to defund, eliminate, and reduce the size of even the most deserving of these agencies, which do more to restrict our personal liberties than they do to enhance our security. Tyranny is the ultimate end of the growth of these agencies; it comes, not suddenly, but gradually over many decades.

The final words of Thomas Paine in *Common Sense* seem an appropriate way to end here, "Until independence is declared, the continent will feel itself like a man who continues putting off some unpleasant business from day to day, yet knows it must be done, hates to set about it, wishes it over, and is continually haunted with the thoughts of its necessity."

Call to Action

Common Sense Rekindled uses reason to persuade readers to act now to rejuvenate the American Experiment. The body of the work provides no action plan, and therefore may be perceived as little more than an academic paper. Such a perception can solve none of today's social and economic problems. Action steps are detailed in this Call to Action.

No action plan will please all sides; an unending search for the best can become the enemy of the good. WWII's General George Patton said that "A good solution applied with vigor now is better than a perfect solution applied ten minutes later." Few readers will agree with all of the action plan points below; some are easy, many are difficult. It is important to seek solutions that protect the conscience of all citizens while preserving the Union established in the 18th century. Not all of Paine's calls to action were accepted, but his recommendations gave political leaders a point of departure; in like manner, the recommendations herein can provide a 21st century point of departure.

Common Sense Rekindled

Recommit to the Moral & Civic Virtue Call of the American Founding

- Re-endorse Spiritual Liberty as essential for Moral & Virtuous Living
    - Active and public, not passive and private
    - Absolute, not relative, moral standards
    - Secular Morality impossible; religious principles form foundation
- Define and build upon moral and ethical principles of Christian Biblical virtues
    - Adjusted by Theistic Rational reasoning
        - Use the Judeo Christian Bible's moral lessons, not its spiritual or literal lessons
        - Extract commonalities that "all good and reasonable men, regardless of faith or no faith, can agree upon."
        - Accept all religious moral beliefs not in conflict with those Judeo Christian moral and ethical principles
- Re-endorse the Founders' principle that America's Republic requires a moral and religious people
    - Political Liberty is possible only with Spiritual Liberty
    - To encourage good conduct as a virtuous citizen
        - Encourage schools to educate citizens in moral and ethical precepts
        - Transform citizens from self-centeredness to other-centeredness
            - Reflected by love & charity to others

- Virtuous citizens are masters of government, not its servants.
- Encourage active religious practice & religious education of citizens
  - Reject extremes of secularism and theocracy.
  - Protect religious liberty from suppression in the public square.
  - Apply 1787 Northwest Ordinance to encourage religious education

Recognize & Accept Enlightenment's Impact on America's Founding

- Search for Truth using reason and faith, not faith alone
  - o Apply Judeo Christian Moral Teachings to life
  - o Reject political theocracy, but not strong religious faith
- Apply Natural Law principles and Judeo Christian moral & ethical principles
  - o To define the "character" of the United States
  - o Focus on general rules of natural law, observable in nature, not on exceptions
  - o Define Natural Rights
    - ▪ Life, Liberty, Pursuit of Happiness, all people created equal
    - ▪ Unalienable because granted by man's creator, not by man

Recommit to the Founders' Federalism of Limited Government Powers

- Focus on preamble of Declaration of Independence, not on list of usurpations
  - Study John Locke's impact on the Declaration
    - Locke's liberal democratic theory (social contract) + Christian morality
      - The "hybrid religion" of America
- Re-confirm that government is to secure peoples' rights, not grant rights to them
  - Lawmakers are elected by the people, not appointed by the Chief Executive
    - Reject that a select group of unelected intellectuals is empowered to make the laws
- Rewrite the 85 Federalist Papers in modern English style
  - Create educational programs to help citizens understand the Founders' original intent in their creation of the federal government's Republican structure
  - Educate citizens on their rights and responsibilities as citizens
- Study Federalist Papers to understand Founders' intent with respect to the Constitution's Articles I, II, and III.
  - Commit to retain this system of separation of powers and checks and balances
    - In particular, ensure Chief Executive Powers do not overpower legislative and judicial powers, particularly in the Executive Agencies.

- Create an Amendment that voids the 17th Amendment to return to the States the rights intended for states which became null with the 17th Amendment
  - The people are represented in the House; the states in the Senate

Recommit to Core Principles in the Preambles of the Declaration of Independence and the Constitution

- All people are created equal with unalienable rights to life, liberty, and the pursuit of happiness
  - Collective rights are subordinate to individual rights
  - Freedom does not mean equality of outcomes, income, or wealth.
- Government is designed to secure, not to grant, these unalienable rights
- The People are sovereign, not servants of the Federal Government.
  - Reconfirm the Constitutional Republican principles of separation of powers and checks and balances, with the Constitution a bulwark, not a fetter.
- Reject philosophy that government and society are too complex for the average citizen's understanding, necessitating a "scientific expert administration."

Reject Progressive and Liberal Progressive Core Principles

- Moral relativism, multiculturism, post-modernism, and the philosophies of Hegel, Nietzsche, Marx, Darwin, Wilson, Croly, Goodnow, and Dewey.
- Pure Democracy and European Socialist model as "best practice."
- Programs that discourage and disincentivize work.
- Expansion of the Constitution's "general welfare" and "necessary and proper" clauses.
- FDR's "Second Bill of Rights."
- Economic statism, including socialism and economic fascism
- Secularism & attacks on America's Judeo Christian culture and Christianity in general.
- Social justice rather than blind justice.
- Equality of outcome, redistributive policies, and economic security over opportunity.
- Welfare for all but those who cannot work at any job.
- Mandates to states in exchange for infrastructure transfer payments.
- Government instead of churches, social organizations, and other private organizations to care for the poor, widows, and orphans to implement "social justice and welfare."
- Progressive and Liberal Progressive call for a federal "Living Constitution"

Implement Fiscal Policies to Reduce Debt & Eliminate Annual Deficits

- Debt no greater than 50% of GDP.
    - o Reduce the numerator and increase the denominator.
    - o To raise GDP, the denominator, emphasize business creation and expansion and significant reduction of regulatory, employment, and taxation burdens
- Conduct a top to bottom review of all executive department agencies
    - o Eliminate or reduce to small & limited scope; return responsibility for most business of executive agencies to the States.
    - o Restrict federal agencies to the writing and implementation of regulations to laws passed by Congress; eliminate their judicial power.
- Only military spending should be allowed to create deficit spending & increase debt
- Repeal laws that require large social spending, such as the LBJ Great Society and War on Poverty programs, which have cost far more than the outcomes they've achieved.
- Review all entitlement programs and eliminate or reduce significantly the programs

Celebrate American Exceptionalism

- Reject intellectuals who denigrate America's exceptionalism and who rewrite history books that portray an evil, uncaring, and selfish Imperialist America.
- Encourage those who have achieved success to share their time, talent and treasure to help others rise to their own success.
- Help the less fortunate learn the "how" of success and the skills so they can rise above their current level, not with a handout but with a hand up and not by lowering the rewards of success but by raising the hopes of success.

Invest Time, Talent, and Treasure in Our Nation's Youth

- Become volunteer youth leaders in churches, schools, scouts, veteran organizations, and other organizations that provide opportunities to transmit our nation's spiritual, moral, ethical, and historical values to our youth, our nation's future political, business, and non-profit leaders.
- Invest your time, talent, and treasure in more than just your family's youth.
- Do NOT "retire" from your duty to serve our youth just because you have retired from the work force.

Acknowledgements

Inspiration for writing comes from many sources. In the case of this work, such inspiration has come primarily from the writings of others. The author's quest for knowledge about America's culture, identity, and history began with confusion arising from reading newspapers, magazines, and online publications, listening to commentators on TV and radio, and listening to other citizens' complaints about the state of the Union.

The common thread of this plethora of information was the United States Constitution. Regardless of the position taken on current day political issues, everyone on all sides of the issue believes that their argument is the constitutionally correct argument. Everyone cannot be correct. This led the author to a search for a deeper knowledge of the U. S. Constitution than mere recitation of the words of an Amendment or of a clause in the body of the Constitution itself.

Such a search is not linear; it twists and turns. It is complex, taking one thousands of years into history rather than just 250 years. And, the search continues on beyond the writing of a manuscript at a single point in time.

A cover-to-cover study of the Bible, to include footnotes, where much of the context of the verses is explained, began before this quest was undertaken. But, the Bible proved its importance, especially the Old Testament, because 18th century and current day conflicts can be put into longer-term historical perspective. The 18th century and current day conflicts, arguments, and divisions are nothing new; history repeats.

The New Testament also proved invaluable because all our nation's Founding Fathers were raised in Christian homes and brought the principles of Christian morality and virtue with them to their State meeting houses and ultimately to the 1787 Constitutional Convention. While their personal lives didn't always meet the high Christian standards, those standards strongly influenced what they decided. Since all were members of Protestant denominations, each of them also brought to the meeting houses the essence of the Protestant Ethic – individualism, hard work, thrift.

In the author's quest for knowledge of what America was designed to be, many sources proved invaluable. Soon after the quest began, Constituting America began a series of annual courses on the Constitution. The annual 90 day studies focused on the Federalist Papers, the Constitution itself, the Constitutional Amendments, and The Classics that Inspired the Constitution. Much of what was learned in those four courses weaves its way through this writing.

Soon after Constituting America began its studies, Hillsdale College began offering online study programs on the Constitution. Hillsdale's Constitution 101 and 201 were important inputs to the author's understanding of America's founding and subsequent Constitutional challenges. Chapter 2 of this work draws almost exclusively on the readings and study guides of Constitution 201.

The Declaration of Independence, the Constitution and Amendments, the 85 Federalist Papers, and Thomas Paine's timely 1776 classic, Common Sense, were read and reread in conjunction with every other reading. Miracle at Philadelphia, by Catherine Drinker Bowen, provided valuable insight into the extreme difficulty of reaching consensus in the hot summer days of 1787.

Thomas Jefferson was the primary author of the Declaration of Independence and James Madison was the primary author of the Constitution. Their correspondence is important to a full understanding of both documents, as well as the relationship of the Constitution to the Declaration. Many people consider them separate documents, which they are physically. However, the core principles of the Declaration's preamble strongly influenced the Constitution. Constituting America's scholars and Hillsdale's faculty showed the relationship in their respective courses.

The author struggled with Chapter 1 until reading *The Religious Beliefs of America's Founders* by Gregg L. Frazer and *An Anxious Age* by Joseph Bottum. The author's conclusions and recommendations in Chapter 1 were strongly influenced by these books.

Portions of Howard Zinn's textbook, *A People's History of the United States*, were read to understand what many college professors today believe about United States' history and what they teach their students. Some attempt to understand the alternative view of America is important to understand the depth of discontent of those who wish to "fundamentally transform" the nation, to include the nation's Constitution.

Other written sources also provided input; this writing was not intended to be a peer-reviewed paper, complete with footnotes and bibliography. Its intent is to wake up a nation of people who are enjoying the fruits of what came from the sacrifices of many over the past several hundred years, including more than 1.3 million Americans who died in combat to preserve what we have for future generations. We now have what others have bled and sacrificed for, and we've become comfortable, safe, and risk averse. It is at times like these, in the history of the world, that true cultural risk is highest; many a great nation has basked in the comfort of success and failed to return to their core values just when those core values were important to keep the nation from falling into an abyss.

The author does not profess to have the ultimate solution to America's ongoing cultural divide. History tells us that answers have a way of rising to the surface only under extreme duress; America is not under extreme duress in 2016. Some of the ideas and action items in this writing may provide ideas for political leaders today; some others may rise to the surface only if and when America reaches a point of extreme duress; and others may not be workable at all at any time.

It seemed time, though, for a revisit to Paine's Common Sense, and a rekindling of the American Spirit of 1776 to keep America from beginning to fall into the abyss. Let's keep the spirit of 1776 alive and rediscover our core values so we can tell Ben Franklin that we've done what he said would be difficult to do, maintain "a Republic, if you can keep it."

Acknowledgements

Made in the USA
Lexington, KY
10 December 2016